PLAYING FUNK RHYTHM GUITAR

BY CHRIS HUNT

Recording by Chris Hunt

Cover art by Levin Pfeufer

Cherry Lane Music Company
Educational Director/Project Supervisor: Susan Poliniak
Director of Publications: Mark Phillips

ISBN 1-57560-542-2

Visit our website at www.cherrylane.com

Table of Contents

Introduction

We all know when we're listening to a good rhythm guitar part. It just feels right. The guitar is making a creative contribution to the song, and it is locked in with the drums. You could say that rhythm is all about "feel" and "time." The goal of this book is to give you the tools you need to get inside "rhythm" as it applies to playing funk and R&B guitar. Through listening to and analyzing recorded examples, this book teaches practical techniques that can take your rhythm guitar playing to the next level. This book uses rhythmic notation, but don't worry if you can't read music—as long as you can count, you can learn this material. Remember that some of the greatest, funkiest rhythm guitar players have never read a note.

TRACK 64

Note: Track 64 contains tuning pitches.

About the Author

Chris Hunt is a New York City–based guitarist, composer, and producer. He has worked with Eddie Kendricks, the Average White Band, Joan Osborne, Martha Reeves, Mary Wells, Taylor Dayne, Brian Howe, Jocelyn Brown, Queen Esther Marrow, Amber, and the Harlem Gospel Singers, among others. He can also be heard on numerous jingles, including those for Cheerios, No Excuses jeans, Sheraton Hotels, and Miller Lite. A graduate of Columbia University, Chris studied guitar and composition at the Berklee College of Music, and with Barry Galbraith and Joe Pass. In addition to being a performing and recording artist, Chris is a sought-after guitar teacher with over 20 years of teaching experience. His CD *Slippery Slope* is available on Amazon.com, and he can be contacted at FourLaneMusic@aol.com.

Acknowledgments

Many thanks to my friends at Cherry Lane—John, Mark, and Susan—and to all my students, past and present, for keeping me on my toes.

This book is dedicated to Elaine, Vivi, and Willow, my soul mates.

Chapter 1—Rhythm 101

For the purposes of this book, we will work with *common time*, also known by the time signature 4/4. In common time, there are four *quarter note* beats per measure. A *half note* takes up the same amount of space as two quarter notes, or is half as long as a full measure in 4/4 time. A *whole note* takes up the same amount of space as four quarter notes, or two half notes, or an entire measure of 4/4 time.

In music, time is finite. That is, in 4/4 time there can never be more than four quarter note beats in a measure. So, if we want more rhythmic possibilities, we must split each quarter note beat in two to get two *eighth notes*.

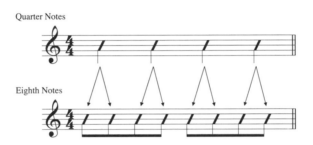

In the musical universe, this division of notes goes on and on. Eighth notes can also be split in half to yield *16th notes*.

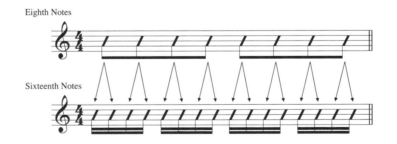

And so on.

The *tempo* (speed) of a song has as much to say about what kinds of rhythms are appropriate as does the style of music. Sixteenth note guitar rhythms don't always sound better than quarter note rhythms. What works best is a matter of context and personal taste. Let your ears guide you.

Chapter 2—Quarter Note Patterns

This first example has a lot of whole note rhythms with a few quarter notes added. It is a relatively uninteresting part, but it can be just the thing needed when there are some very rhythmically active horns, keyboards, or other guitars to contend with. This is a very simple strumming pattern. Think of it as down–up–down–up (one strum for each quarter note beat). Be sure, however, *not* to strum in the right places; these "phantom strums" are set off in this book by parentheses. On these phantom strums, pull your strumming hand away slightly from the strings, making sure to pull it back in again for the strums you *do* want to play. Maintaining this back-and-forth motion can greatly help you to keep in time.

TRACK 01

TRACK 56
Play-Along

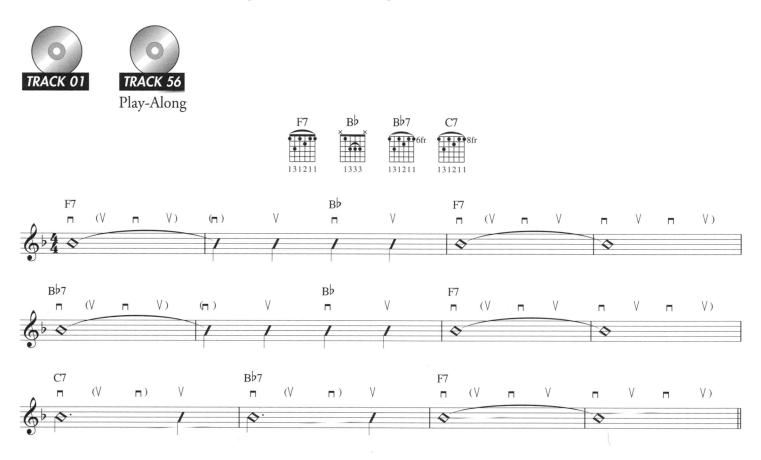

Notice that there are *two* tracks listed for many of the examples in this book. The first one is always the actual music as it's written, so you can hear what an example sounds like before you try to play it. The "Play-Along" track indicated is just that—a recording with bass and drums (but no rhythm guitar) to which you can "play along."

This next example reinforces beats 2 and 4, or the *backbeat.* The backbeat is the very backbone of R&B. In fact, if you never play anything but beats 2 and 4, you'll almost never go wrong! Notice that the left hand releases its grip early, giving a staccato effect. This is a technique you will hear throughout the CD.

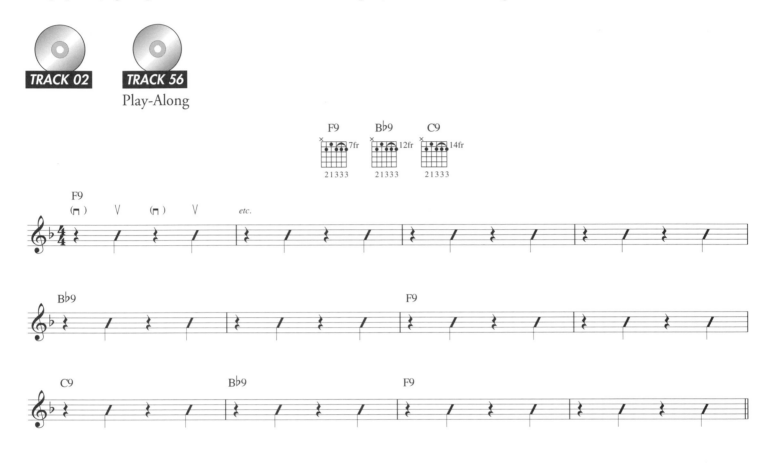

Here is the backbeat in a reggae context.

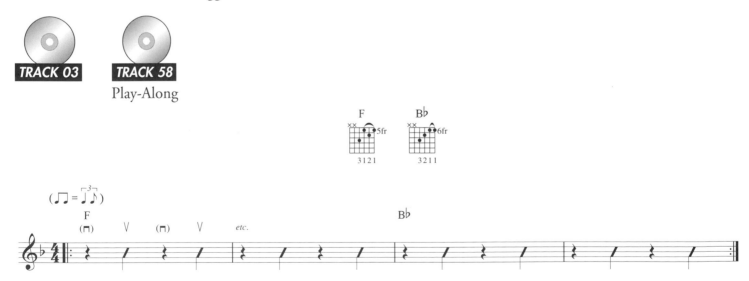

In this next example, the backbeat is played over a shuffle blues.

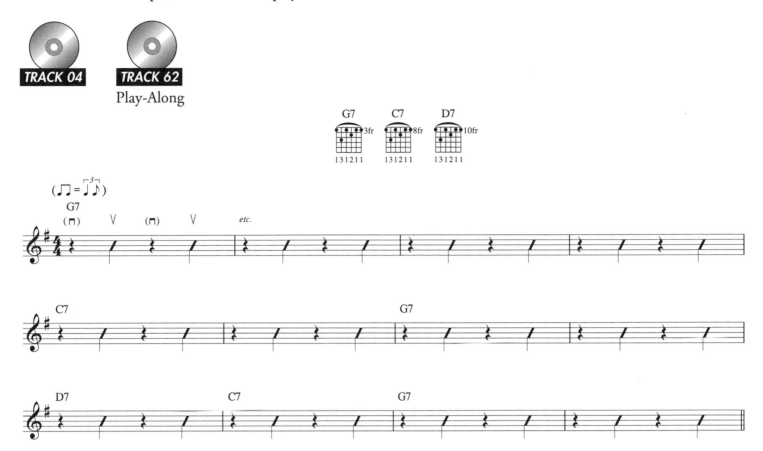

Chapter 3—Eighth Note Patterns

This is a good opportunity to introduce a classic eighth note rhythm. Each one of these articulations is an upstroke, but the muted downstrokes really propel the thing along. To muffle the strings, simply release your fretting hand slightly. Always remember that your right hand is the timekeeper. As long as your stroke is steady and constant, you'll be in the pocket.

TRACK 05

TRACK 62
Play-Along

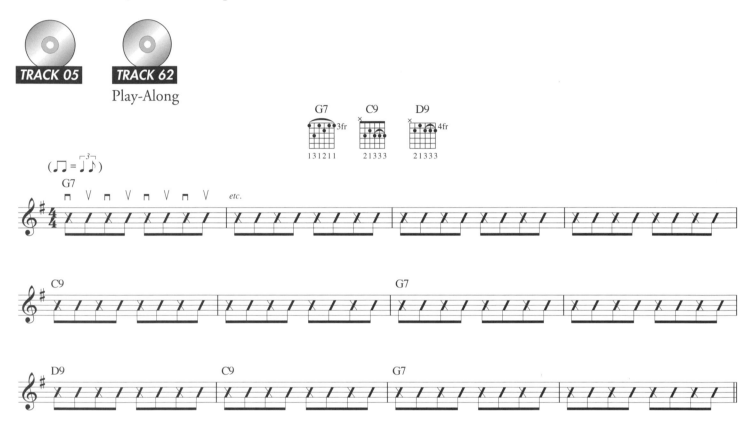

Here, you should retain the steady eighth note strum, but the articulations come on the downbeat of 1 and the upbeat of 2.

TRACK 06

TRACK 62
Play-Along

This is the very same rhythm in a different context.

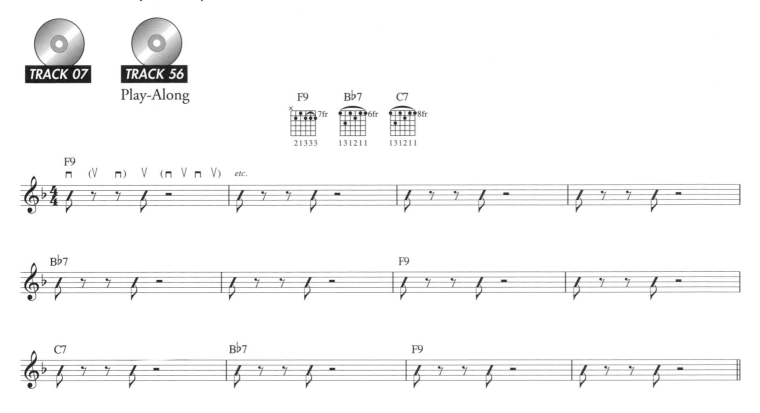

This eighth note rhythm makes use of a slide into beat 2. Although the "phantom strokes" aren't indicated here, don't forget to include them to help you keep time.

Play-Along

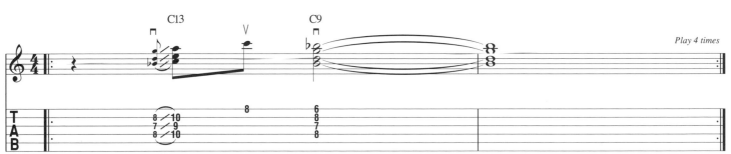

Chapter 4—Sixteenth Note Patterns

And now—the 16th note strum. Again, you should always keep time with that right hand. This is a really good rhythm to practice for consistency. The chord here is one you may not be familiar with. Check it out.

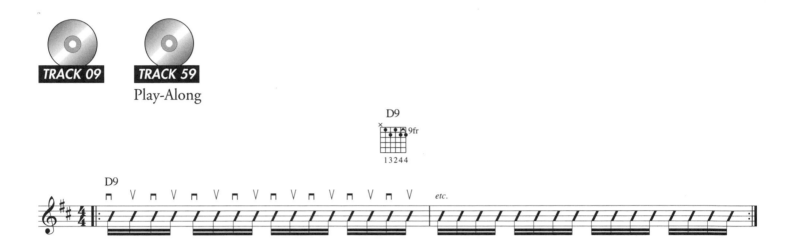

This example shows how eloquent a 16th note strum can be due to the many choices that are possible. The muting of strokes is a really important part of rhythm playing. It accomplishes two things: it keeps you in time by not breaking the momentum, and adds a kind of "guitar percussion" effect.

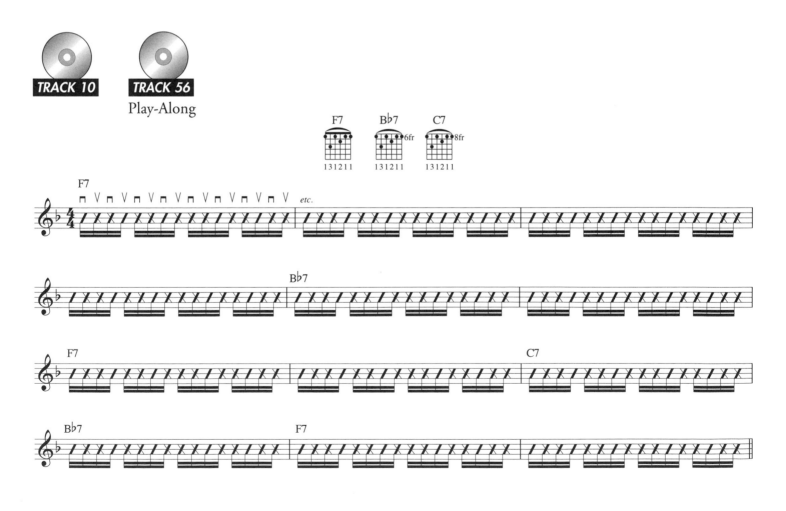

Here is a similar rhythm.

TRACK 11

TRACK 59
Play-Along

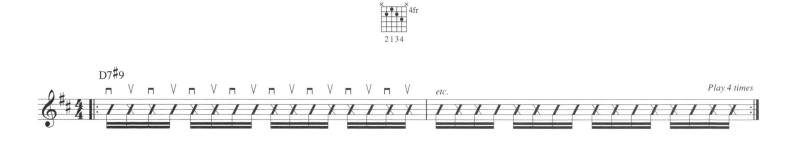

This example is also a 16th note strum with muted articulations. The chord riff here is known as a *minor cliché*, and it will often work over a minor chord.

TRACK 12

TRACK 57
Play-Along

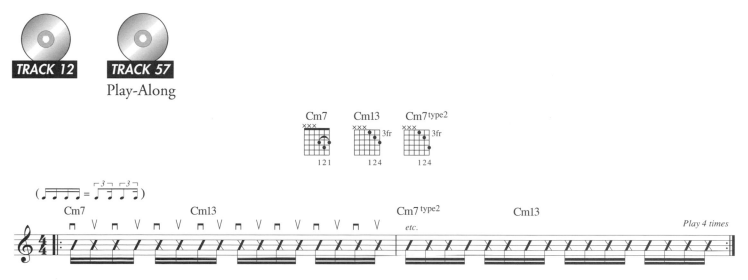

Here are two more versatile rhythms.

TRACK 13

TRACK 57
Play-Along

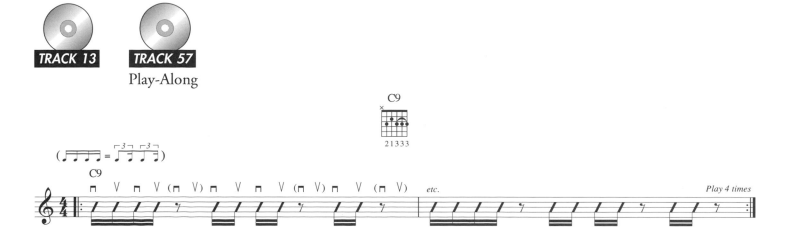

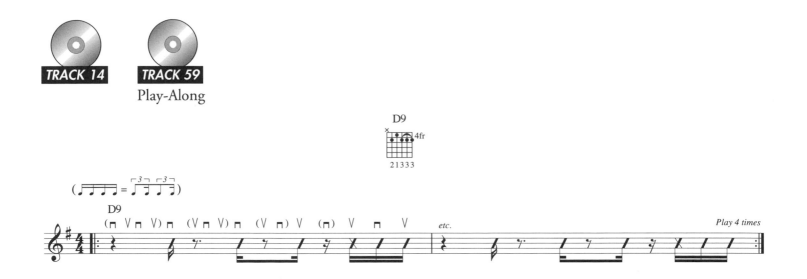

And now, back to a minor key. These 16th note examples feature moving chord schemes that are a bit of a challenge. Each stays within a C minor sound but uses *triads* (three-note chords) to create motion.

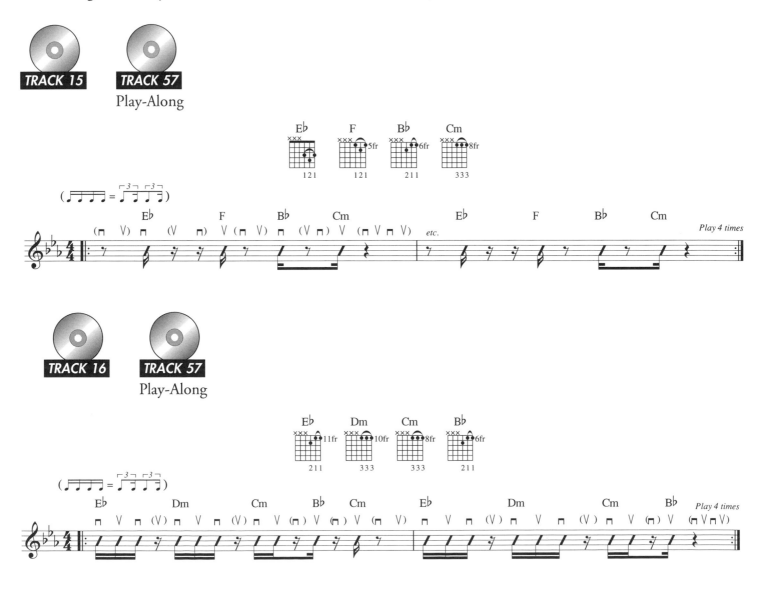

Here is a tight little rhythm derived from a horn line, with a 16th note in only beat 2.

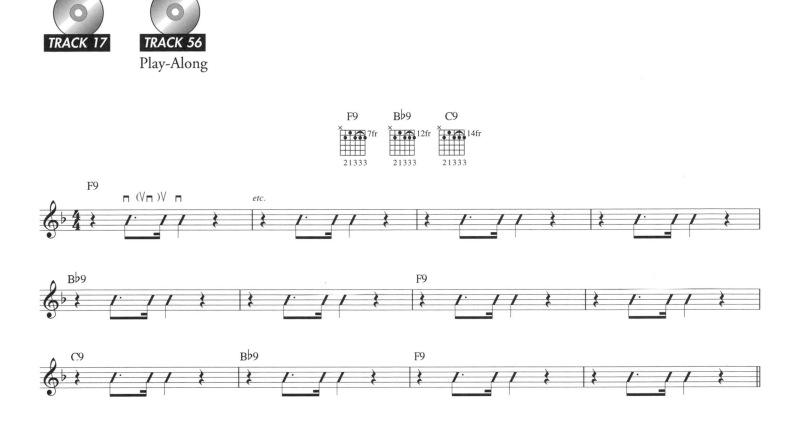

This is the same as the previous example but with a slide into beat 2. Just finger the F9 chord beginning at the 6th fret to get the E9, the Bb9 chord beginning at the 11th fret to get the A9, and the C9 chord at the 13th fret to get the B9—and slide up.

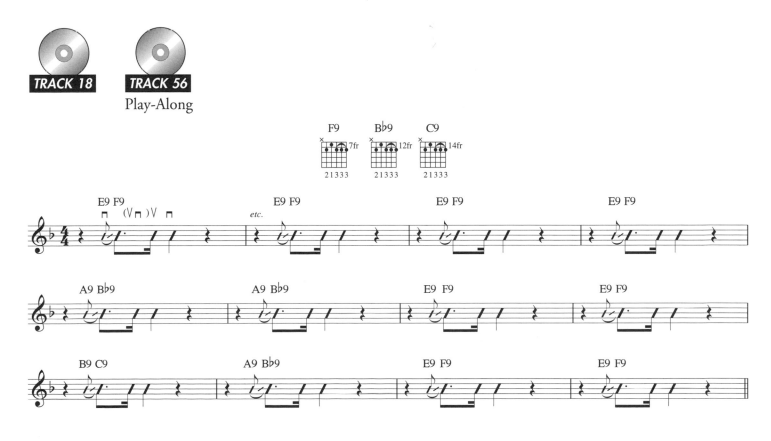

Here, the same rhythm is moved to beat 1.

TRACK 19   **TRACK 56**
Play-Along

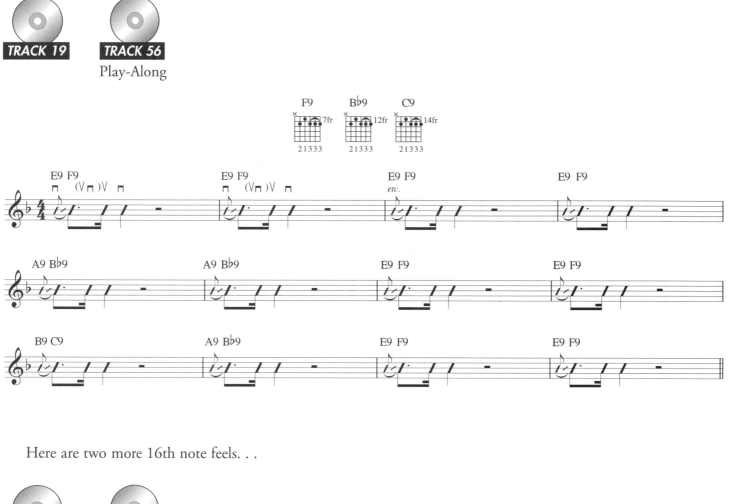

Here are two more 16th note feels. . .

TRACK 20   **TRACK 56**
Play-Along

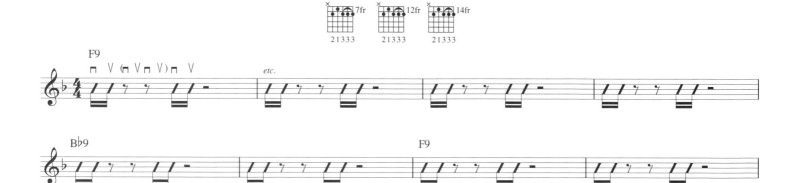

TRACK 21   TRACK 56
Play-Along

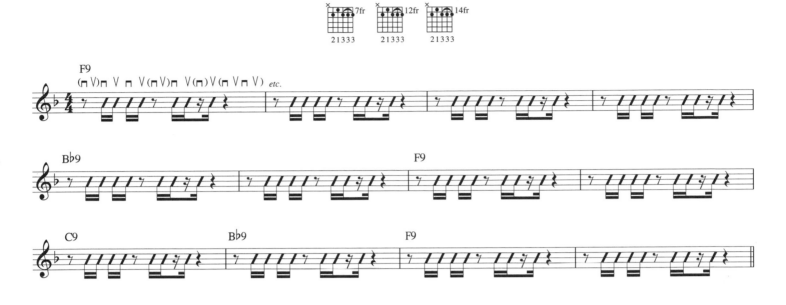

. . . and another example of a rhythm derived from a horn line.

TRACK 22   TRACK 59
Play-Along

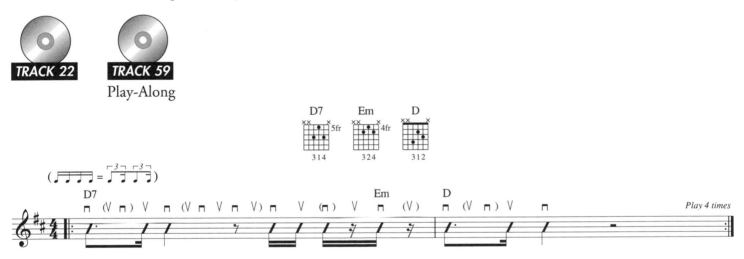

This example employs two different voicings of the same basic chord sound. Notice how the C7 on beat 3 seems to answer the C9.

TRACK 23   TRACK 57
Play-Along

Chapter 5—Triplets

Up until now, we've dealt with even divisions of notes, but any note can also be divided into three equal parts. The result is called a *triplet*. When you play three eighth note triplets for each beat, you end up with 12 eighth notes in each measure, or what's called a *12/8 feel*.

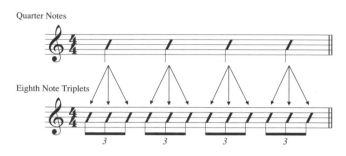

Here are three variations on a theme.

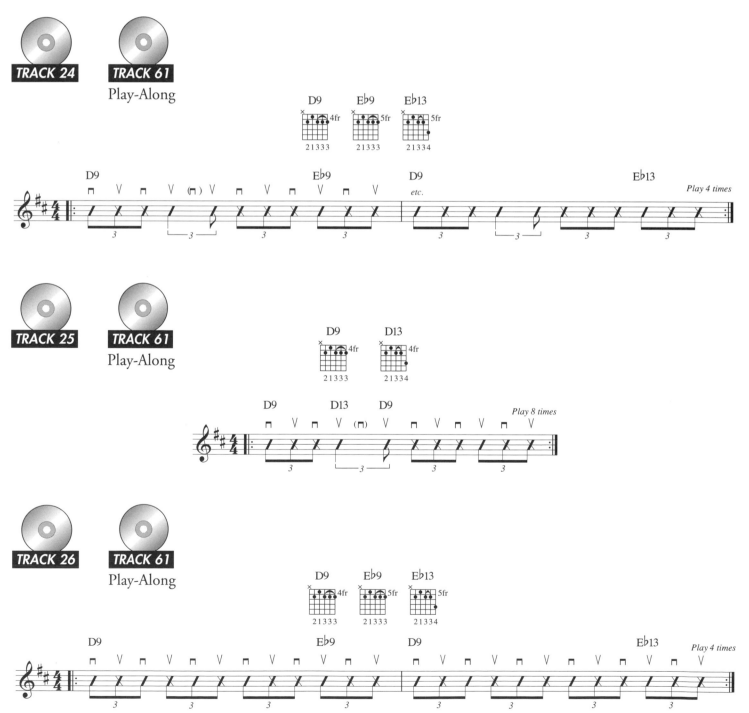

This example features a really useful minor 9th voicing. Notice how nicely the high E string cuts through the rhythm section.

Play-Along

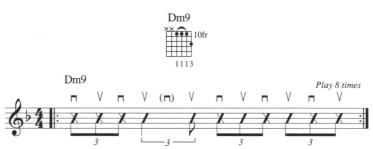

This chord riff falls right into the D minor pentatonic box.

TRACK 28   TRACK 61

Play-Along

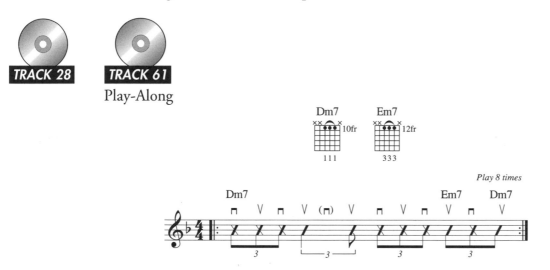

Here, the 12/8 guitar rhythm dances over a shuffle groove.

TRACK 29   TRACK 62

Play-Along

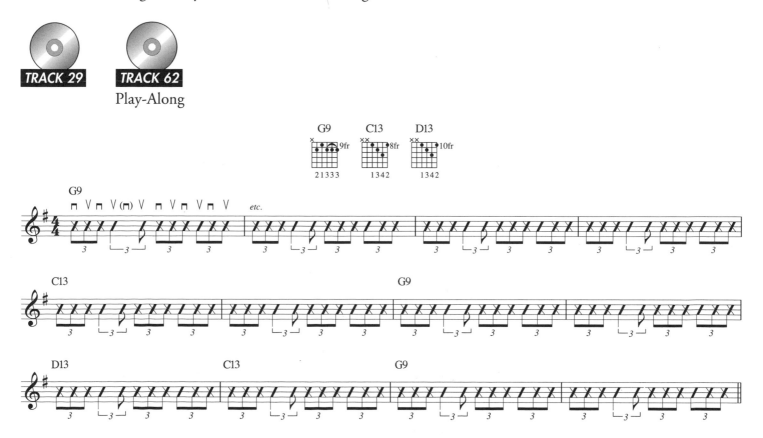

This groove is so slow that I added eighth note triplets to the count-off.

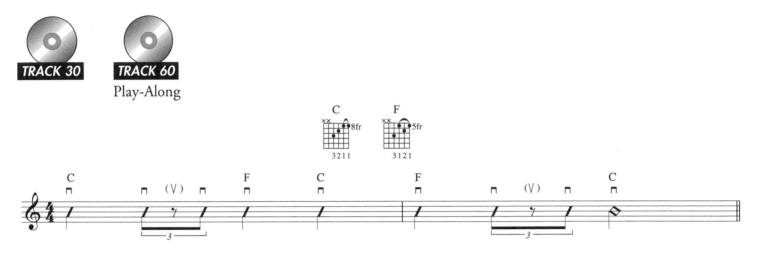

Because the tempo is slow for this next one (there are eighth note triplets in the count-off again), you can easily split each eighth note into two 16th notes for more rhythmic possibilities. Now, you can play six notes (16th note triplets) per beat. Even though for this example the 16th notes occur only on beat 1 of each bar—and I've left out the "phantom strums" for a bit of a challenge—keep the strum going. It may seem like wasted effort, but it keeps you in position for more choices. In time, your right hand will develop a kind of "memory" that will allow you to just jump in at any place with the right strum in any rhythm, and these phantom strokes will become unnecessary.

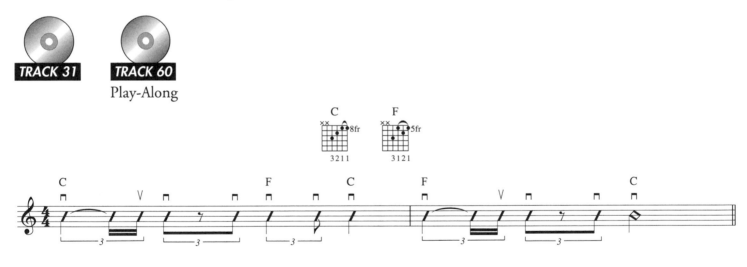

This is a variation of the previous example. Here, passing chords break things up a little.

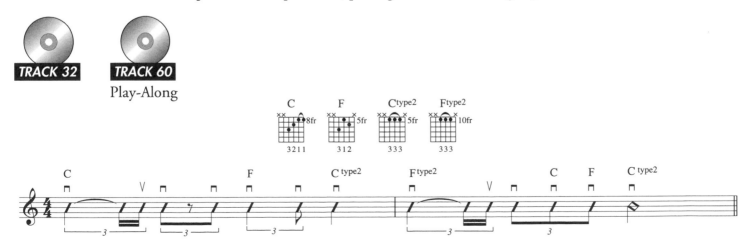

This slow example takes a more melodic approach and also makes use of triads.

 TRACK 33   TRACK 60
Play-Along

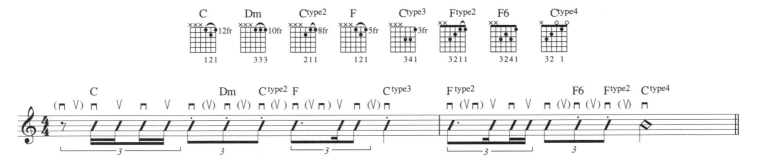

This is an example of a full-blown triplet pattern. Each note in each eighth note triplet has been split into three for a total of nine notes per quarter note beat. This has a very African flavor.

TRACK 34   TRACK 60
Play-Along

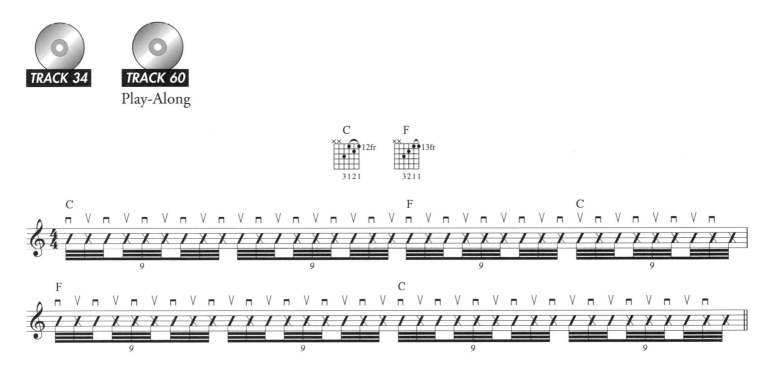

Chapter 6—Single-Line Rhythms

Sometimes the most effective rhythm guitar part is a single melodic line. It usually works best when there is a keyboard taking up a lot of space.

This is a funky little rhythm that sounds a lot like a clavinet part.

TRACK 35

TRACK 57
Play-Along

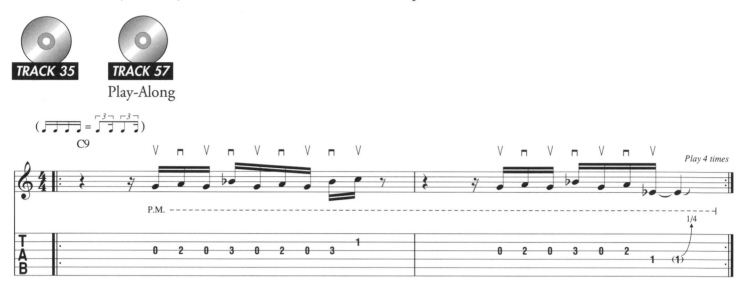

Here is a single-line rhythm derived from a minor pentatonic scale.

TRACK 36

TRACK 59
Play-Along

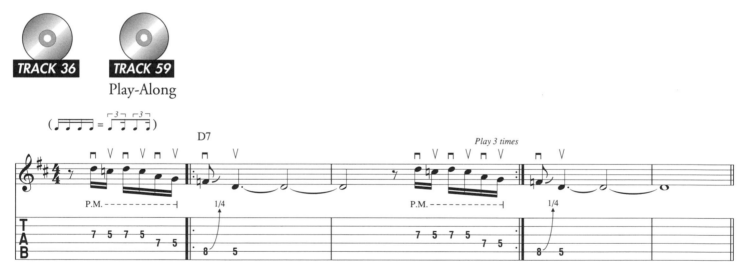

In this example, a single line rhythm sounds big due to the playing of muted strings.

TRACK 37

TRACK 59
Play-Along

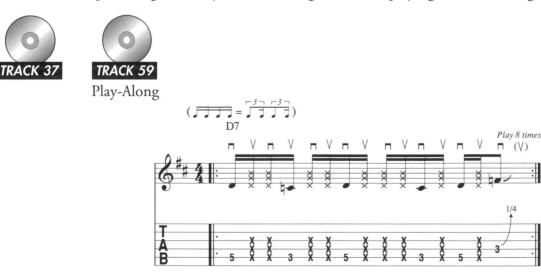

Chapter 7—Mixed Examples

This chapter features rhythm patterns that utilize all of the techniques we've covered in this book, but the examples don't fit neatly into categories. For instance, a single example might be comprised of an eighth note pattern and a 16th note pattern.

Below, beat 2 contains a dotted eighth–16th note pattern, while beats 3 and 4 contain eighth note patterns.

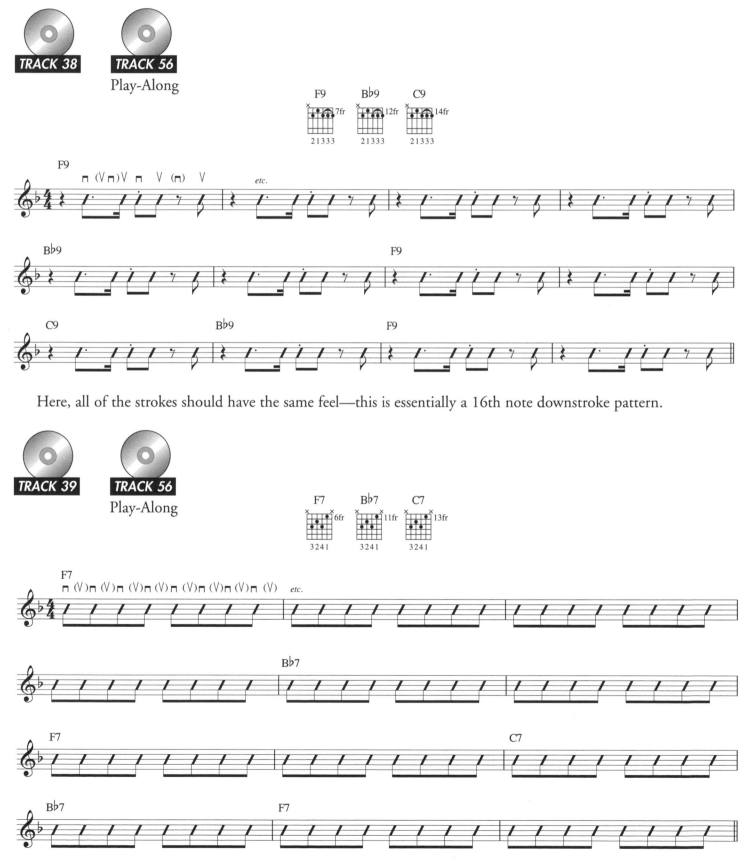

Here, all of the strokes should have the same feel—this is essentially a 16th note downstroke pattern.

Here is the same part with some actual 16th notes added.

TRACK 40 **TRACK 56**
Play-Along

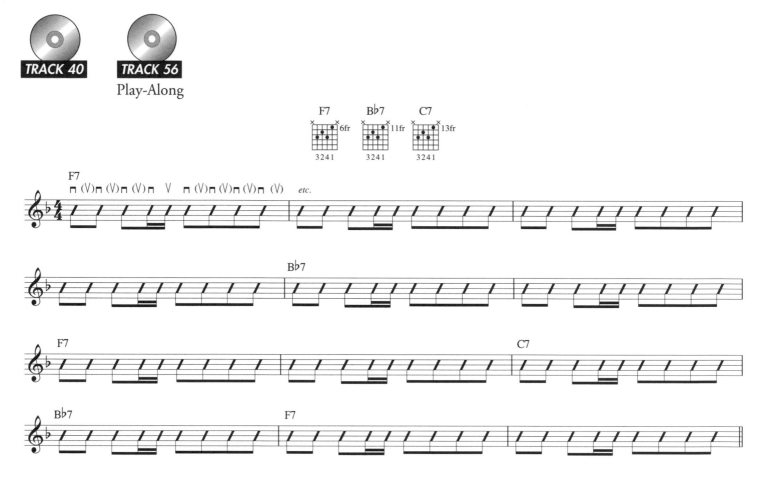

Beats 2 and 3 here get an eighth note pattern.

TRACK 41 **TRACK 57**
Play-Along

Here's a 16th note single-line pattern with a double stop in beat 4.

TRACK 42   TRACK 57
Play-Along

This example is made up of mostly a 16th note feel.

TRACK 43   TRACK 57
Play-Along

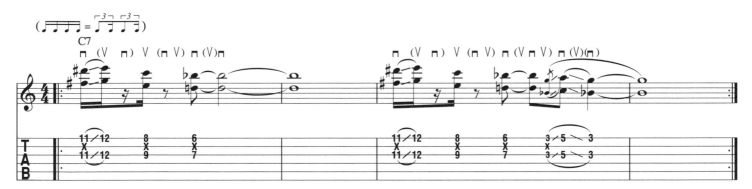

Here's an example with mostly an eighth note feel with some pick-up notes.

TRACK 44   TRACK 59
Play-Along

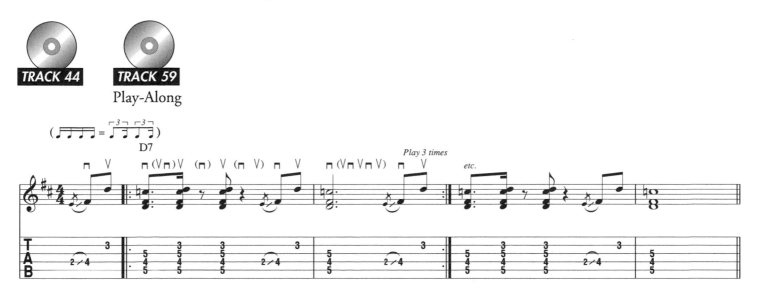

This example contains a 16th note pattern on beat 1 and eighth notes on beats 2, 3, and 4.

This one has a lot of flavor. The quarter note triplets make it a little difficult to sight-read, so really use your ears on this one.

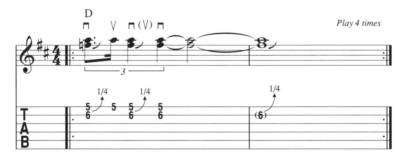

Here's a good mix of 16th and eighth notes.

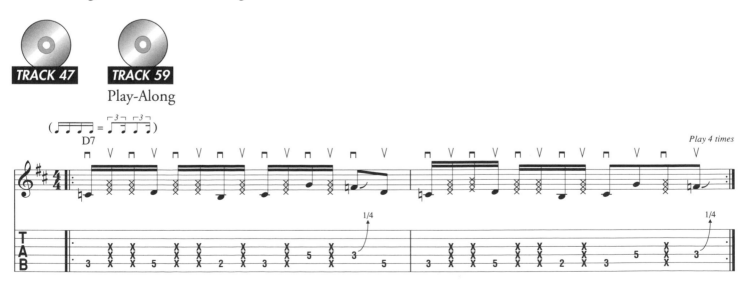

Let's revisit the reggae groove—this time, with some characteristic eighth and quarter note patterns.

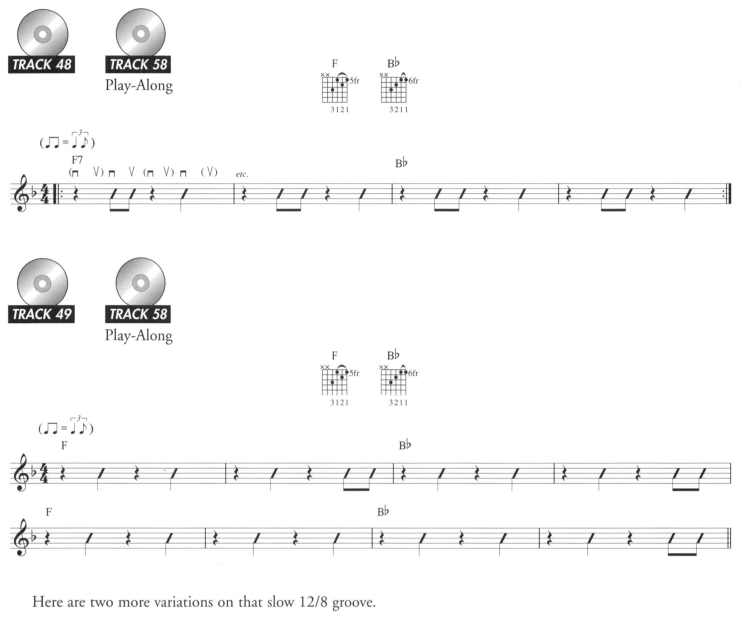

Here are two more variations on that slow 12/8 groove.

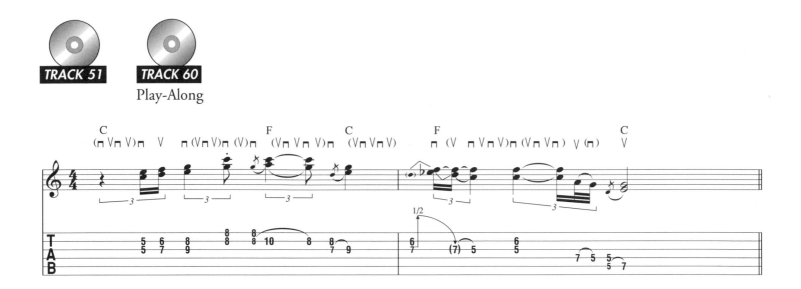

TRACK 51 **TRACK 60**
Play-Along

These two patterns have some very nice (and functional) chord voicings that you may wish to incorporate into your playing.

TRACK 52 **TRACK 62**
Play-Along

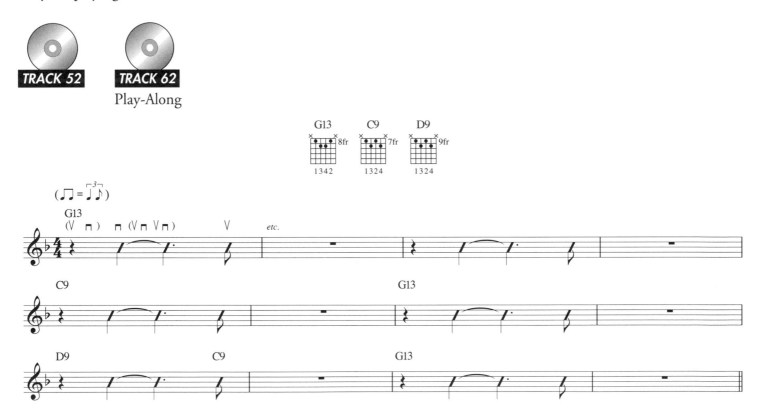

TRACK 53   TRACK 62
            Play-Along

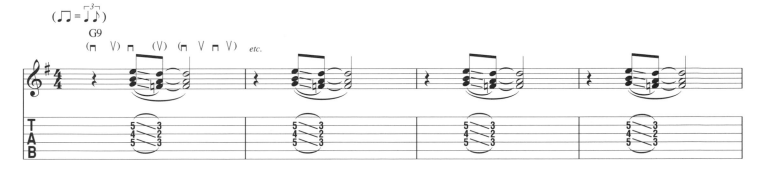

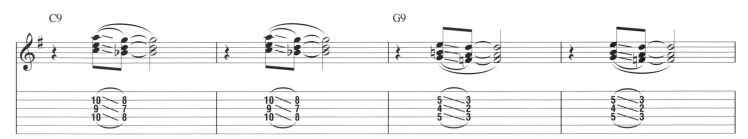

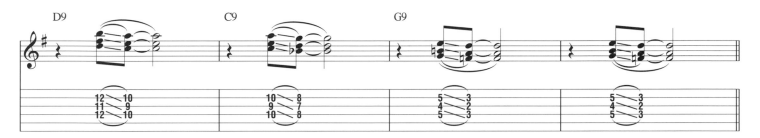

Here are two different takes on a pop R&B tune. In the first there's a mostly-muted, single line part, and in the second there's more of a straight rhythm.

TRACK 54   TRACK 63
            Play-Along

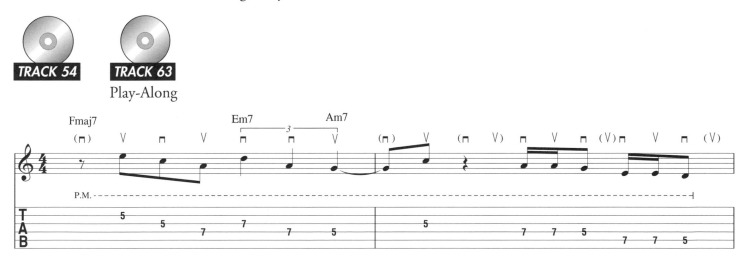

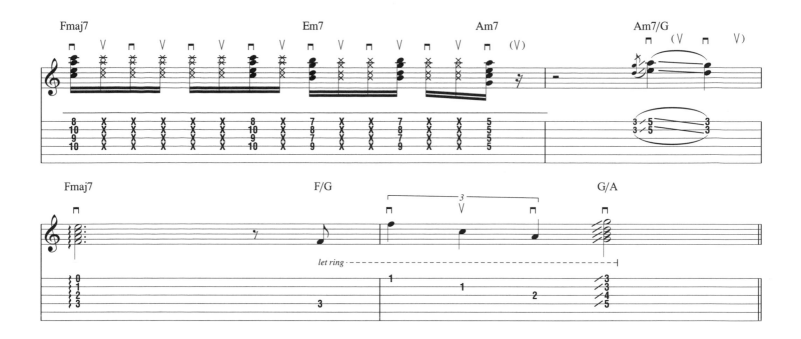

GREAT STEELY DAN BOOKS

from **CHERRY LANE MUSIC COMPANY**

STEELY DAN'S GREATEST SONGS
15 more trademark Steely Dan songs, including: Aja • Chain Lightning • Daddy Don't Live in That New York City No More • Everyone's Gone to the Movies • Haitian Divorce • Josie • Pretzel Logic • Reeling in the Years • and more.
02500168 Play-It-Like-It-Is Guitar $19.95

BEST OF STEELY DAN FOR SOLO GUITAR
11 great solos, including: Aja • Babylon Sisters • Deacon Blues • Doctor Wu • Gaucho • Haitian Divorce • Hey Nineteen • Kid Charlemagne • Peg • Rikki Don't Lose That Number • Third World Man.
02500169 Solo Guitar...$12.95

BEST OF STEELY DAN FOR DRUMS
10 classic songs for drums from Steely Dan. Includes: Aja • Babylon Sisters • The Fez • Peg • Two Against Nature • Time Out of Mind • What a Shame About Me • and more.
02500312 Drums $18.95

STEELY DAN LEGENDARY LICKS (GUITAR)
28 extensive musical examples from: Aja • Babylon Sisters • Black Cow • Bodhisattva • Josie • Kid Charlemagne • Parker's Band • Peg • Reeling in the Years • Rikki Don't Lose That Number • and many more.
02500160 Guitar Book/CD Pack...$19.95

STEELY DAN JUST THE RIFFS FOR GUITAR
by Rich Zurkowski
More than 40 hot licks from Steely Dan. Includes: Babylon Sisters • Black Friday • The Boston Rag • Deacon Blues • Kid Charlemagne • King of the World • Peg • Reeling in the Years • Rikki Don't Lose That Number • Sign in Stranger • and more.
02500159 Just the Riffs – Guitar...$19.95

THE ART OF STEELY DAN (KEYBOARD)
Features over 30 great Steely Dan tunes for piano: Aja • Black Cow • Bodhisattva • Hey Nineteen • I.G.Y. (What a Beautiful World) • Parker's Band • Reeling in the Years • Third World Man • Your Gold Teeth II • many more.
02500171 Piano Solo $19.95

STEELY DAN JUST THE RIFFS FOR KEYBOARD
28 keyboard riffs, including: Babylon Sisters • The Boston Rag • Deacon Blues • Don't Take Me Alive • Green Earrings • Hey Nineteen • Peg • Reeling in the Years • Rikki Don't Lose That Number • and more.
02500164 Just the Riffs – Keyboard $9.95

BEST OF STEELY DAN
A fantastic collection of 15 hits showcasing the sophisticated sounds of Steely Dan. Includes: Babylon Sisters • Bad Sneakers • Deacon Blues • Do It Again • FM • Here at the Western World • Hey Nineteen • I.G.Y. (What a Beautiful World) • Josie • Kid Charlemagne • My Old School • Peg • Reeling in the Years • Rikki Don't Lose That Number • Time out of Mind.
02500165 Piano/Vocal/Guitar..$14.95

STEELY DAN – ANTHOLOGY
A comprehensive collection of 30 of their biggest hits, including: Aja • Big Noise, New York • Black Cow • Black Friday • Bodhisattva • Deacon Blues • Do It Again • Everyone's Gone to the Movies • FM • Gaucho • Hey Nineteen • Josie • Reeling in the Years • more!
02500166 Piano/Vocal/Guitar..$17.95

BEST OF STEELY DAN FOR GUITAR
15 transcriptions of Steely Dan's jazz/rock tunes, including: Bad Sneakers • Black Friday • The Boston Rag • Deacon Blues • FM • Green Earrings • Kid Charlemagne • Parker's Band • Peg • Rikki Don't Lose That Number • Third World Man • Time Out of Mind • and more.
02500167 Play-It-Like-It-Is Guitar $19.95

Prices, contents, and availability subject to change without notice.

CHERRY LANE MUSIC COMPANY
6 East 32nd Street, New York, NY 10016

EXCLUSIVELY DISTRIBUTED BY

HAL•LEONARD CORPORATION
7777 W. BLUEMOUND RD. P.O. BOX 13819 MILWAUKEE, WI 53213

http://www.halleonard.com

0401